AS English Language & Literature
UNIT 1

AQA

Specification B

Module 1: Introduction to Language and Literature Study

John Shuttleworth

Philip Allan Updates
Market Place
Deddington
Oxfordshire
OX15 0SE

Orders

Bookpoint Ltd, 130 Milton Park, Abingdon, Oxfordshire, OX14 4SB
tel: 01235 827720
fax: 01235 400454
e-mail: uk.orders@bookpoint.co.uk
Lines are open 9.00 a.m.–5.00 p.m., Monday to Saturday, with a 24-hour message answering service. You can also order through the Philip Allan Updates website: www.philipallan.co.uk

ISBN-13: 978-1-84489-030-9
ISBN-10: 1-84489-030-9

This guide has been written specifically to support students preparing for the AQA Specification B English Language and Literature Unit 1 examination. The content has been neither approved nor endorsed by AQA and remains the sole responsibility of the author.

Printed by MPG Books, Bodmin

Philip Allan Updates' policy is to use papers that are natural, renewable and recyclable products and made from wood grown in sustainable forests. The logging and manufacturing processes are expected to conform to the environmental regulations of the country of origin.

AS English Language & Literature

Contents

Introduction

■ ■ ■

Content Guidance

■ ■ ■

Questions and Answers

Introduction

About this guide

The aim of this guide is to help you prepare for the **Unit 1: Introduction to Language and Literature Study** examination — the first module of the AS English Language and Literature (AQA B specification). It is intended as a revision aid and to show you how to prepare yourself effectively for the unit exam. It is not, however, a textbook for the unit. There are three sections to the guide:

- **Introduction** — this explains exactly what you are required to do for the unit and outlines the format of the exam, which is based on a short *Anthology* of themed texts. The theme of the 2006–08 *Anthology* is *Town and Country*.
- **Content Guidance** — this section provides a guide to the integrated study of language and literature that lies at the heart of the specification and this unit. It offers advice about the ideas and approaches required to be successful in the unit and suggests ways of ensuring that you write a successful answer to exam questions.
- **Questions and Answers** — this section includes examples of typical questions that you will encounter in the Unit 1 exam. This is followed by examples of A-, C-, D- and U-grade candidate answers. These are interspersed with commentaries from the examiner which highlight the strengths and weaknesses of each answer.

It is hoped that by working carefully through this guide you will feel confident of obtaining a high mark in your exam.

Studying English Language and Literature

In the study of English Language and Literature it is important to be reassured that you are not studying two separate subjects. You may have some friends who are taking English Language A-level and some who are taking English Literature A-level and wonder why you have to take both. You may feel disadvantaged in that you think you are taking both subjects and getting just one A-level for your pains. This is emphatically not the case. You do not have to 'learn' as much English Language as them, nor as much English Literature, for only half the rewards. English Language and Literature in this specification is a totally different subject from either English Language or English Literature. Nor does the specification take a bit from the English Language course and add it to a bit from the English Literature course and call the result English Language and Literature. Therefore, you cannot say when studying parts of your AS course: 'Ah! Now I'm doing the Language bit and now I'm doing the Literature bit.'

The whole idea that underpins the specification and therefore Unit 1 is that the study of language and literature is integrated, not divided into separate parts. Those texts that are called 'literary' use language to communicate to their audience and to achieve their purposes, just as do those spoken and written texts which are (most unhelpfully) labelled 'non-literary'. It is the basic philosophy of the subject you are studying that exploring and examining how a writer (or, indeed, a speaker) uses language in *any* text can illuminate its meaning in the best possible way. The idea that there is a special language of literature or a special literary style that is divorced from real language use is not always a helpful one. To give you just one example of what is meant by this: spoken language and talk are a feature of communication in everyday life; people talk to each other all the time. It is therefore possible for linguists to study how talk works in such everyday situations. They can examine, for example, how new topics are introduced into a discussion or how people can take different roles within a conversation. The study of everyday talk in all its aspects is a fascinating one and you may well already have been introduced to it in this unit. But talk also figures large in those texts that are labelled 'literary'. There is a lot of talk (sometimes called 'dialogue') in novels and short stories and, of course, talk is almost always the main constituent of plays.

Many of the ways that talk in everyday life can be studied are helpful also in showing us how a dramatist can, for instance, create a character or achieve a particular dramatic effect. For example, you can examine what the relationship is between Othello and Desdemona at a particular point in the play by looking at the words he uses to address her. What does he call her? Is it always the same throughout the scene? What do these 'address terms' (as linguists call them) tell the audience about his feelings for her at this point? And just as you can learn something about the characters and their relationships in a play by looking at 'address terms' in everyday conversations, you can also infer something about the relationship between those speakers. The important difference to remember is that, while speakers in real life are themselves in charge of what they say, in plays and novels it is the writer who decides for his or her own particular literary purposes what the characters will say. This brief example should clarify what is meant by saying that this specification *integrates* the study of language and literature.

Principles of Unit 1

The title of the unit should give you an indication of its aims: *Introduction to Language and Literature Study*. By the time you have finished your work on Unit 1 and are preparing for the exam, you will have encountered all the important issues that are covered in the remainder of the specification. You will have read and studied in depth a small number of significant texts which have been specially chosen to enable you to focus on these issues and to give you experience of reading a variety of texts by different authors, of different genres or types, and which have a variety of purposes. You will have studied texts that have traditionally been called 'literary', such as extracts from prose fiction, from drama and from poetry. You will have studied texts that have traditionally been called 'non-literary' (though this label seems to imply that they are somehow the 'second-class citizens' of the textual world, when, in fact, they are nothing of the sort) and, it is to be hoped, you will have realised that this distinction can be somewhat arbitrary and unhelpful. You will have studied texts that are intended to be spoken or, indeed, are transcripts of real speech and you will also have read texts that were produced in times earlier than our own. In other words, you will have read texts of the type and variety that you will meet in the other units of the course.

Links with other units

Here it is shown briefly how the work you have done for Unit 1 has prepared you for your work on the remaining units of the specification.

Unit 2: The Changing Language of Literature (AS)

Your study of extracts from prose fiction that were written in modern times and ones from earlier periods will prepare you for work on this unit in which you will study two complete, short novels that are related by theme, but which were written at least 100 years apart.

Unit 3: Production of Texts (AS)

Your study of the texts in Unit 1 introduces you to the notion of different text types (or genres) and to the fact that texts can have different purposes and different audiences. These factors have a major influence on the way that writers or speakers choose their language to communicate most effectively with their audience and to achieve their purposes. This study of audience, purpose and genre will prepare you for the coursework unit, Unit 3, in which you have to draft and write two texts that are aimed at different audiences, written for different purposes and in different genres. Your work on spoken language will also help you to prepare for the fact that one of your two pieces must be for a listening audience.

Unit 4: Text Transformation (A2)

Your study of prose fiction, poetry and drama together with an associated emphasis on different genres will prepare you for work on the second coursework unit in the specification, in which you will take a literary text of your choice and transform it into, or adapt it for, a genre other than the one in which it was originally written.

Unit 5: Talk in Life and Literature (A2)

Your study of spoken texts (both spontaneous and scripted) will prepare you for this unit in which you explore the ways that writers of prose fiction, drama and poetry use features of everyday talk to create dramatic or literary effects.

Unit 6: Critical Approaches (A2)

Your study of a number of different texts, all related by a common theme, will prepare you for this unit in which you will be given a short anthology of texts, again related by a common theme, a few days before the exam. You are expected to explore these texts on your own and to demonstrate your understanding of them by comparing them in ways of your own devising.

The *Anthology*

The basis for your work in Unit 1 is a short *Anthology* of themed texts. In a sense, you can regard it as your set book. Some of you will be familiar with using an anthology for an exam as many GCSE specifications also have them. As all the questions in the exam for this unit are based on texts from the *Anthology*, it is probably a good idea for you to know what the principles are that form the basis of your *Anthology*. What are the reasons for the selection of the texts that you must study?

Each *Anthology* has a theme and all the texts are chosen because they have connections with this theme. The theme for the *Anthology* that you are studying is *Town and Country* and it will form the basis of exam questions for three years from 2006. The *Anthology* for subsequent exams will have a new theme and a new set of texts.

Each *Anthology* is divided into two sections. Section One consists of a short selection of poems, written either by one single poet or by a small number of poets. In the *Town and Country Anthology*, all the poems in Section One are written by the American twentieth-century poet Robert Frost. All the poems in this section deal in some way with nature, landscape and country life. By considering this section carefully, you are also fulfilling one of the requirements for Language and Literature specifications: that you must study poetry.

Section Two consists of texts concerned with towns or cities and urban life. These texts exemplify the variety of text types that you will encounter later in the specification. Thus, there are prose texts, both fiction and non-fiction, drama texts (including one short yet complete play by Harold Pinter), one short poem about London and examples of both scripted and unscripted speech. The genres that are represented in Section Two include novels, autobiographies, diaries, political speeches and an extract from the Bible. The writers (and speakers) of these texts all have differing attitudes towards their chosen towns or cities. Charles Dickens, for example, is critical of the industrial town of Preston, which he disguises as Coketown in the extract from *Hard Times*, whereas the speaker in the extract from Rohinton Mistry's *Family Matters*, Yezad, is much more affectionate towards his home town of Mumbai (Bombay).

There is also a short introduction that provides you with some contextual information about each of the texts in Section Two. This is important as it provides you with some background designed to help you understand the texts more fully. Context will be considered again in more detail in the Content Guidance section.

Assessment objectives

Your exam paper is marked according to assessment objectives (AOs). These are the criteria that the examination board uses when assessing your work in English Language and Literature. Thus, your examiners have to judge the skills, knowledge and understanding you have shown in your answers in the light of these assessment objectives. The AOs for this unit are listed in the table on p. 8.

AO1	Communicate clearly the knowledge, understanding and insights gained from the combination of literary and linguistic study, using appropriate terminology and accurate written expression.
AO2	In responding to literary and non-literary texts, distinguish, describe and interpret variation in meaning and form.
AO3	Respond to and analyse texts, using literary and linguistic concepts and approaches.
AO4	Show understanding of the ways contextual variation and choices of form, style and vocabulary shape the meanings of texts.
AO5	Identify and consider the ways attitudes and values are created and conveyed in speech and writing.

Assessment objectives, such as these to be used for Unit 1, can appear dry and forbidding for students, and even for teachers and examiners, too. In the next sections of this guide, they will be explained and interpreted to show how you can meet these objectives in your answers.

There is no need to worry about the AOs. The questions that you will face in the exam for Unit 1 have been carefully written and checked to ensure that they meet these assessment objectives. So the advice that you will have been given by teachers in every exam subject, whether it be SATs or GCSEs, still holds good for this exam: 'Answer the question that is set'. If you read the question carefully (including any bullet points which will have been included to help and guide you) and do exactly what the question tells you to do, then you will have no problem in meeting these seemingly daunting assessment objectives. Of course, if you do not do as the question requires, you are unlikely to fulfil the assessment objectives, with predictable consequences for your mark. Examiners can award good marks only to scripts that do in fact answer the question that has been asked. They mark your work by considering the relevance of your answer and your engagement with the texts you have chosen.

The exam

Unit 1 is assessed by a written exam lasting 1 hour and 30 minutes, which is worth 35% of the total AS mark, and 17½% of the total A-level mark.

The exam consists of two questions, both of which are compulsory. Question 1 is on the poems in Section One of the *Anthology*; question 2 is on the texts in Section Two of the *Anthology*. Each question requires you to write on *two* texts.

Both questions are worth 35 marks, so you must allocate your time carefully. One way of using the exam time might be to spend:
- 45 minutes on each question *of which*
  - 10 minutes is spent making notes and planning your answer to each question *and*
  - 35 minutes is spent writing your answer to each question, *therefore*
- 17½ minutes is spent writing on each text in the questions

If you keep to this strict time allocation, you will gain a higher mark than you would if you spent longer on one or two of the four texts, just because you felt more confident about them. Examiners expect you to devote an equal amount of attention to each of the four texts that you choose to write about and they assess your answers accordingly.

Question 1

This question focuses on the poems in Section One of the *Anthology*. You must write on two poems, one of which has been chosen for you by the examiner. You therefore have to select the second poem and it is absolutely vital that you choose one that is relevant to the question. Candidates lose many, and sometimes all, of their marks if an inappropriate poem is chosen.

The question will ask you to focus on an idea or theme about which, in the case of the present *Anthology*, Robert Frost writes. For example, a recent question asked candidates to show how Frost writes about 'time and change' in 'The Oven Bird' and in one other poem. You can therefore see that if your own choice of poem is not about 'time and change', you will lose marks.

There are usually two bullet points as part of the question as well. These are there to guide you and to help you to write relevantly. They are usually as follows:

> You should write about:
> • how the language used conveys [the poet's] ideas
> • form, structure and organisation

The focus of these bullet points is the poet's use of language, his or her choice of form (whether the poem is a sonnet or a dramatic monologue, for example) and the way in which the ideas and themes are organised within the poem.

So, to ensure success in question 1, you must:

• choose a second poem that deals with the same themes and ideas as the examiner's choice
• explain clearly what the poet is saying about these themes or ideas in each poem
• explain how *some* of his choices of language help to communicate these themes or ideas
• explain clearly how the ideas are structured and organised in the poem

You can see from this that the emphasis in the question is on the poet's *methods* and *ideas*. Remember, too, that the question does *not* ask you to compare nor contrast the two poems.

Question 2

This question focuses on the texts in Section Two of the *Anthology*. Unlike question 1, however, the examiner does not select either of the texts that you have to write about. You must choose both texts yourself, so it is important that you select appropriate and relevant texts. Choose wrongly and you could forfeit most of your marks.

A further difference from question 1 is that whereas the focus of that question is on the poet's ideas and the way that he or she uses language to communicate these ideas, the focus of question 2 is more on the writer's (or speaker's) crafting and techniques, though, of course, the way that language is used in the texts will form part of your answer. Crafting a text obviously involves a writer making choices about how he or she is going to use language.

For instance, recent questions have focused on the ways in which a writer (or speaker) creates a character, tells a story or produces humour. You will have to consider the content of your chosen texts, but the main focus of your answer must be on the methods the writers employ to achieve these effects. You are also expected to know something of the context of the texts in Section Two, as this knowledge will help you to understand them more fully. This point will be explored further in the Content Guidance section, but it is not an onerous requirement. Another difference between questions 1 and 2 is that there are usually no bullet points in question 2 to give you guidance on how to structure your answer.

So, to ensure success in question 2, you must:
- choose *two* texts that will enable you to answer the question relevantly
- refrain from summarising or paraphrasing the content of your chosen texts
- focus clearly throughout your answer on what the question is asking

Keys to success

The basic ways to ensure success in the Unit 1 exam are straightforward. First, you need to *know all the texts in both sections of the* Anthology *thoroughly*. If you are not familiar with any of them or have not prepared them properly, then you may easily be caught out in the exam by an unexpected question.

Second, you should *read the questions carefully to see **exactly** what the examiner is asking* and ensure that you answer on what is required, not on what you hoped would be the question. Remember, an examiner can give your answer marks only if it is relevant, however insightful it might have been. The examiner has to be fair to all those candidates who did answer relevantly.

Third, you must *choose the texts you are going to answer on carefully* to ensure that they allow you to focus on the issues that the examiner wants you to write about. Appropriate choice of texts is essential for success.

Finally, a word of reassurance. Your examiners are not looking to penalise you at every possible opportunity and deduct as many marks as they can. They enjoy marking good, focused and relevant answers and would love to give you full marks, but they can do so only if you follow the advice that your teachers have given you and which forms the basis of this guide. If you are well prepared, then the exam and its examiners will hold no fear for you.

Content
Guidance

This section covers the key terms and concepts with which you need to be familiar for the Unit 1 exam. It also gives you advice on how to approach the exam itself.

It begins with an explanation of the important frameworks for both language and literature study before considering and defining the key terms used by examiners in question 1 and question 2. A clear understanding of these terms will help you to focus your exam answer more effectively.

The section continues with suggestions as to how you can best prepare yourself for taking the Unit 1 exam, before concluding with advice on how to ensure that your exam answers are successful.

Working with texts

The essence of this specification is that the study of literature and of language is an integrated one and not one that is a combination of two separate disciplines.

Traditionally, some types of text have been labelled as 'literary' and some labelled as 'non-literary'. In the former category are novels, short stories, poetry and drama. The latter category has customarily been much larger, containing all the remaining types of text that have not been given the accolade of 'literary' — a sort of second-class citizenship — for example, sports reports, insurance policies, textbooks, washing instructions, guidebooks and exam answers. It has come to be recognised that this black-and-white distinction between 'literary' and 'non-literary' is not a satisfactory one. Where, for example, do you put autobiographies, diaries, television comedy scripts, advertisements...? It is probably much easier therefore to consider that you are working with texts of all types and not to worry too much about distinctions that can at times prove problematic. If you respond to the texts you are asked to deal with by demonstrating a critical awareness of the way in which the writer or speaker uses language to construct and convey meaning and marry this with an understanding of relevant contextual and cultural factors, then you are doing all that your examiners require.

The neat but somewhat unsatisfactory division of texts into 'literary' and 'non-literary' can be mirrored by a further division of texts into 'spoken' and 'written'. Many texts are clearly 'spoken' ones — everyday conversations, telephone calls, consultations between doctors and patients, for instance — and many are clearly 'written' — novels, insurance policies and newspaper articles. There are some, however, that are more problematic to categorise. Is the language used in an internet chat room spoken or written? Some advertisements try hard to give the impression that you, the potential consumer, are being spoken to in a friendly way and some political speeches have been carefully written and crafted to give the impression of impromptu delivery. As a result, this division of texts into 'spoken' and 'written' that appears so commonsensical on the surface can also raise some interesting problems.

The criteria for English Language and Literature specifications do refer to literary and non-literary texts and to spoken and written texts; from your point of view as a candidate for this unit all you need to do is to deal with the texts you are presented with in your *Anthology* and on your exam paper and not to worry about these distinctions into categories.

We will now look at the ways in which examiners expect you to respond to the variety of texts that you have encountered during your work on Unit 1 and on the exam paper itself.

Frameworks

'Frameworks' is a term often used by teachers and examiners when discussing the various ways in which texts can be considered and explored. They sometimes speak of 'language frameworks' or 'literary frameworks'. This section looks at some of these frameworks.

The term 'frameworks' can be rather daunting, suggesting a mechanical way of exploring a text. Remember that what your examiners want you to do when you are looking at a text is not only to show that you understand what the writer (or speaker) is saying, but also to demonstrate that you can see *how* the meaning of the text has been created and conveyed. To do this, you have to be able to discuss the way in which he or she uses language, and your examiners will look to see if you have approached this task in a systematic manner. The use of frameworks should allow you to do just this.

Language is an interlocking system of words and sounds. To convey meaning these words and sounds need to be linked in a systematic way. If, for example, words were just written down in a random order ('black loudly swiftly the the into cat ran dog pursued house a by barking' instead of 'the black cat ran swiftly into the house pursued by a loudly barking dog') then it would be only with great difficulty that we could unravel the meaning. There are various components to the language system and words and sounds are only two of them. However, it is possible to separate out these various components and each one is sometimes referred to as a 'framework'. So, when you are exploring how a writer (or speaker) has created meaning (say, by looking at the types of words he or she has chosen), you are using a framework.

Remember, however, that the overall meaning of a text is created by the writer using a combination of frameworks and that to separate them out for discussion is only part of your task. You need to see how they work in combination to create meaning.

Bear in mind, too, that you should not use these frameworks as a checklist worked through mechanically for every text you encounter. You need to be selective. For example, the 'sound framework' (phonology) may not be at all important in helping to create meaning in some texts. You have to decide which are the appropriate ones to use in a particular text.

Note that it is not enough merely to identify some of the features of the language of a text. Not only should the features you select to write about be significant, but you should also include some discussion, exploration and interpretation of them in your answer.

Some key frameworks

Each framework is followed by a brief definition of its scope and then a list of some key features associated with that particular framework. *These key features are not intended to be comprehensive, but to give you an indication of the features that can be discussed within a particular framework.*

Lexis: the words, phrases and idioms of language

Key features *may* include:
- the choice of words (e.g. simple, complex, slang, clichéd, abstract, concrete, everyday, specialised, old-fashioned etc.)
- how formal or informal
- the types of words that predominate

Grammar: the structure of units of language no longer than the sentence

Key features *may* include:
- long or short sentences
- types and functions of sentences (statements, commands, questions, exclamations)
- sentence structure (simple, compound, complex, minor)
- features of the verb
- phrases and clauses
- word classes (nouns, verbs, adjectives, adverbs etc.)
- word order

Phonology: the sound patterns of language

Key features *may* include:
- characteristics of normal speech (volume, stress, intonation, pauses, fillers etc.)
- sound patterns usually associated with rhetorical or literary texts (rhyme, rhythm, assonance, consonance, alliteration, onomatopoeia etc.)

Semantics: the meaning of language

Key features *may* include:
- semantic fields
- types of meaning (positive/negative, specific/vague, literal/figurative)
- contrasts in meaning
- imagery and figurative language (metaphor, simile, personification, puns, exaggeration, understatement etc.)

Graphology: the visual appearance of language

Key features *may* include:
- print or handwritten
- font type, style, size
- punctuation (used to clarify meaning, to indicate rhythm and other speech features, for rhetorical purposes?)
- colour, logos, captions, diagrams, photos etc.

Discourse: the overall structure and organisation of a text

Key features *may* include:
- written genre (or spoken situation)
- structure and organisation of the text
- how the parts of the text link together

- register (topic, formality, tone)
- relationships between writer/speaker and audience
- management of speech situation (turn taking, agenda setting, topic switches etc.)

Do not worry if you think that these frameworks seem to overemphasise the linguistic approach to your texts. This is not so. Writers of the traditional 'literary' genres (prose fiction, poetry and drama) obviously have to employ language and therefore a close examination of the way in which they use language in such texts will give you not only a clear understanding of the meaning(s) of these texts but also insight into how these meanings are created. Take imagery as just one example. 'Literary' texts, particularly poetry, frequently employ imagery to create and enhance meaning. However, it is only through a close examination of the words used to create the image (or series of images) that you will arrive at a critical understanding of the image and its function in the text and be able to assess its effectiveness. You are likely to have been using a combination of the lexical and semantic frameworks to arrive at your understanding.

A further example is the creation of a character in a novel or a play, often the focus of literary concern. Just how is character created by a novelist? It is usually through a combination of description, the character's own words, actions and relationships with other people in the novel and how other characters speak of and relate to him or her, in addition to the writer's own comments on and assessment of this 'person' — in other words, through language.

A note on terminology

Assessment objective AO1 says that you should be able to demonstrate your ability to:

> Communicate clearly the knowledge, understanding and insights gained from the combination of literary and linguistic study, using appropriate terminology and accurate written expression.

It is therefore important that you communicate clearly the knowledge, understanding and insights that you have gained from your study of a variety of texts. This clarity will depend on the accuracy and precision of your own writing. But what is 'appropriate terminology'? In the section on frameworks you might have found that there were some terms that you have not encountered before and thought that you would be penalised if you did not use them in the exam. This is not the case. Examiners do not expect you to use a specific set of terms and will not penalise you if you do not. Terminology is only a convenient, shorthand way of referring to features of a text and the same language feature can be referred to in a number of different ways.

For instance, take the phrase 'the delicious cake'. The word (by the way, the word 'word' is an example of terminology) 'delicious' in the phrase (more terminology) can be described in a number of ways. Some people might call it an *adjective*, others might call it an *epithet*, whereas others might call it a *pre-modifier* — three different ways of defining the same thing. You may even have been taught other ways of referring to it. The important thing to remember is that examiners do not have a preference for one set of terminology over another. What they want you to do is to refer to your chosen language feature as precisely and accurately as you can. Your answer would be long-winded if you did not have any terminology at your disposal. It would become tedious if you had to refer to 'the word between "the" and "cake"' every time you wanted to write about 'delicious'.

Remember, too, that terminology is only a means to an end. You will gain no credit merely by parading your mastery of terminology. You need to be able to show the effect of your chosen and precisely defined language feature. Some candidates appear to think that if their answers are peppered with abstruse and complex terminology their examiner will be impressed. However, the examiner will be impressed only if you have used the terms accurately and have demonstrated why you think the writer has used these particular language features. The use of terminology for its own sake is inadvisable.

A useful memory jogger: ILEE

Some candidates have found this mnemonic (or memory jogger) useful when preparing to answer questions on texts: ILEE. What do these letters stand for?

Identify

When exam questions ask you to comment on the way in which a writer or speaker has used language in a text, you are not expected to deal with every single feature. Indeed, the amount of time you are allowed to answer a question would prevent you from doing so. You are expected to *identify* some of the significant language features of a text. There are two key words here: *some* and *significant.*

Some should indicate to you that you cannot comment on everything. You must be selective. If you try to comment on every language feature of a particular text, you run the risk of writing superficially. Examiners penalise this sort of answer severely. They call it 'feature-spotting'. It is much better to select a small number of language features and to discuss the result that these features have, in your opinion, and explore in depth the contribution they make to the meaning and effect of the text. You can easily demonstrate your ability as a top-grade candidate by focusing on, say, two or three important or *significant* ways in which a writer or speaker is using language.

Significant should also remind you of the need to be selective when discussing the language of a text. Not every use of language in a text is as important in contributing to the overall meaning and effect as others and, therefore, to achieve the highest marks possible, you should ensure that you select and concentrate on the most significant ones. For instance, candidates often write: 'the writer has used a mixture of compound, complex and simple sentences in this text'. They appear to feel pleased with themselves that they have identified something important and, furthermore, have managed to use some imposing terminology. However, these candidates fail to realise that, in the vast majority of cases, prose writers frequently use such a mixture of sentence types. It may well be an accurate observation about a writer's language use, but it is not a significant one. Far more significant a use of language would be if a candidate noticed that, for instance, a writer concluded his text with a simple three-word sentence, having preceded this final sentence with a series of long and grammatically complex sentences. The candidate would then be able to discuss the effect of this contrast in sentence types and length.

You should comment on only the most significant features of the language of a text. You do not have time in the exam to do more.

Label

This returns to the issue of terminology. When you have selected what you think are the most significant features of language use in a text for comment, it will then save you a lot of time if you are able to label them using the appropriate terminology when discussing them. But remember the warnings given in the preceding section that terminology is only a means to an end, not an end in itself. It is more important for you to be able to identify the significant features and explore them than it is to worry too much about the terminology you are using. Of course, if you can identify important language use and employ the appropriate terminology, so much the better.

Exemplify

Writing down every instance of where a particular language feature is found in a text is a waste of precious exam time. The examiner does not expect you to do so. It is quite sufficient for you to exemplify, giving one or two brief examples of the feature you are discussing — no more. Of course, if you fail to cite any example at all, then the examiner will begin to doubt whether you know what you are talking about. You should aim to strike a balance between giving too many examples and giving none at all.

Explain and Evaluate the Effect

Three *E*s for the price of one here. If you have followed the advice above about identifying, labelling and exemplifying, then you will have done well, but not well enough. If you want to achieve the higher grades, then it is vital that you follow the 3E rule. You need to *explain* (and explore) what you think is the *effect* of a particular language choice on the writer's part. This is where your opinions become important, as there may be no right answers. You may sometimes find it frustrating when you ask your teacher 'What does this mean?' and the response is 'What do you think?' But your teacher is absolutely right to ask you the question, because what an examiner is interested in is not what your teacher or some critic might have said about a particular text, but in what *you* have to say. It is your understanding and response that are crucial, not someone else's. Nor is it important what the examiner might think — he or she may disagree with your view, but if you have argued it strongly and supported it with evidence from the text, then you will be rewarded. By doing this, you are also likely to have covered the third E — *evaluating*. All this requires is that you express a supported opinion on how successful the writer (or speaker) has been in creating and conveying his or her meaning.

Below is a brief and straightforward example of ILEE in action:

> In this text the writer is directly addressing the reader by use of the second person pronoun [identification of a significant feature together with accurate terminology] 'you' in, for example, line 25 (if you walk down to the right…) and again in line 34 (you can see…) [two examples provided]. This creates a friendly and relaxed relationship [discussion of effect] which means that the writer is more likely to be able to persuade the reader to visit the attraction [evaluation].

Unpicking the questions

Question 1

All questions on Section One of the *Anthology* (question 1 on your exam paper) follow the same format. A recent question was:

> Look again at 'The Oven Bird'. With careful reference to this poem and to one other poem from Section One of the *Anthology*, show how Robert Frost writes about time and change.
>
> You should write about:
> - how the language used conveys Frost's ideas
> - Frost's use of structure and organisation

There are a number of things to note about this (and therefore every question 1):
- The examiner has chosen one poem for you to write about.
- You have to choose a second poem (from Section One of the *Anthology*) to write about. It is therefore essential that you choose wisely by selecting one that enables you to address the topic that the examiner has selected. This is discussed in more detail on p. 9.
- The examiner has chosen a theme that he or she thinks can be found in a number of poems by (in this case) Frost. In this question the theme is that of 'time and change'. Your own choice of poem *must* allow you to write about this chosen theme. Therefore, one sensible way of approaching revision for this question is to think of as many themes as you can that Frost writes about and to list all the poems in the *Anthology* in which this theme is covered. This should ensure that your choice of poem is appropriate.
- There are two bullet points to guide and direct your writing. You would be foolish to ignore these bullets.
- The first bullet point focuses on language and ideas. In other words, you are being asked to discuss and explore the way in which Frost uses language to create and convey his feelings and ideas about 'time and change'. The focus of this part of the answer is therefore on two important points. These are, first, what Frost says about 'time and change' and, second, the way in which he expresses these ideas. The bullet point begins with a small but vitally important word: 'how'. This word provides you with the crucial signal that the examiner wants you to write about not only Frost's ideas, but also the methods he uses to communicate them.

- The second bullet focuses on 'structure and organisation'. (Sometimes the word 'structure' is replaced by the word 'form'.) Here you are being asked to look at the poet's choice of poetic form (lyric, sonnet, narrative poem, short pithy poem, for example) and show how this choice of form contributes to the overall effect of the poem. 'Organisation' asks you to write about how the ideas in the poem develop and link together. For example, what is the effect of the use of strongly rhymed couplets in 'Nothing Gold Can Stay'? How do the ideas contained in each couplet link together?

Question 2

Though the wording of question 2 is not as standard as that of question 1, there are some common factors to all of them. Below is a recent question 2:

> Choose *two* texts from Section Two of the *Anthology* in which writers and/or speakers seek to persuade or influence the reader or listener.
>
> How do the writers and/or speakers seek to do so?

There are a number of things to note about this example (and therefore every question 2):

- Here the examiner has not indicated either of the texts that you should write about. You must choose *both* texts yourself. This makes it even more important that you select texts that enable you to answer the question. If you choose unsuitable texts, you will struggle to answer relevantly and the examiner will have difficulty in awarding you any marks.
- The question allows you to choose either texts written for a reading audience or texts spoken for a listening audience. You do not have to choose one spoken and one written text. You are free to choose both from one mode, if it suits your purposes.
- Unlike in question 1, the focus is less on themes and ideas, and more on methods and approaches. The examiner will choose a writer's (or speaker's) objective or purpose and ask you to show how this objective or purpose has been achieved. In this question, for example, the objective or purpose selected is that of persuading or influencing the reader. Previous questions have focused on creating a character, telling a story or creating humour.
- There are usually no bullet points to guide you.
- As with question 1, the focus is on the writer's or speaker's methods. The crucial word 'how' again appears at the start of the question. You ignore it at your peril. There are no marks awarded to candidates who do ignore it and choose merely to paraphrase or summarise the content of their chosen texts.

Context

One of the assessment objectives that question 2 targets is AO4. This states that you should:

> Show understanding of the ways contextual variation and choices of form, style and vocabulary shape the meanings of texts.

This section focuses on 'contextual variation'. Many candidates are puzzled by this phrase and want to know what it means and how much they should include in their answers on the contexts of the texts they are writing about. How much do examiners expect candidates to know about the background to the texts?

There are two main ways to look at context. One is to consider the circumstances that surround a text at the time it was being written or spoken. This is sometimes called the 'context of production'. The other is to consider the circumstances that surround a text when it is being read or heard. This is sometimes called the 'context of reception'.

The main areas that could be included under context of production are as follows:

Audience	The type of reader or listener that the author could expect to encounter the text.
Genre	The type of text that the writer is producing.
Biography	The personal circumstances of the writer or speaker.
Place	Where the text was produced.
History	The political, social and economic circumstances at the time of writing (or speaking).
Culture	The cultural circumstances at the time of writing (or speaking) — these could include, for example, scientific, philosophical or religious thought and, of course, the prevailing literary and linguistic circumstances.

All or some of these contextual factors will have affected the text and the ways that its meanings are created and conveyed, and you need to have some awareness of this.

Naturally, the context of reception will include all of the above and, if the text is read at almost the same time that it was produced, then these contexts are unlikely to cause readers any difficulties. For example, if you read *The Secret Diary of Adrian Mole Aged 13¾* at the time it was published, then the references to Mrs Thatcher and the Falklands War would need no contextual explanation. To read the book some 50 years (or even 20) after publication might require a set of explanatory footnotes. Texts can also be received differently, depending on the context (or circumstances) under which they were read or heard. The national anthem 'God Save the Queen' is received differently at the Conservative Party conference from at the FA Cup final or by listeners to a track on a punk album.

The more distant in time a text is, the more contextual information is needed to understand it fully. The views on witchcraft when Shakespeare was writing *Macbeth*, for instance, are somewhat different to our own. English cities in the seventeenth, eighteenth and nineteenth centuries will have differed considerably in a multitude of ways, as will have people's attitudes to them and such contextual information needs to be borne in mind when reading the texts in Section Two of the *Town and Country Anthology* by Samuel Pepys, Tobias Smollett and Charles Dickens.

It is important, however, for you to get context and contextual variation into perspective. The questions you are asked in Unit 1 focus on either a writer's ideas or purposes in a particular text and on the methods he or she uses to create and express these ideas or purposes. What is *not* required is an answer that tells the examiner, for example, all about the life of the writer or about the historical circumstances when the text was written and ignores what the writer is saying or doing and the methods used to communicate meanings. Contextual information is useful to you in illuminating a text, but it must not be the centre of your answer.

How to prepare for the exam

There are a number of steps you can take to ensure that you are fully prepared for any question that you encounter in the Unit 1 exam.

Examiners sometimes complain that candidates do not seem to know the texts in the *Anthology* well enough. It is assumed by examiners that you will know the content of each text in the *Anthology* thoroughly and where there is evidence that this is not the case, you will lose many marks. The least to expect is that you know what every text is about. If you have attended all the lessons and have paid attention throughout, then you will have no difficulty in fulfilling examiners' expectations in this respect. It is always useful, however, before sitting the exam to remind yourself of the content of the texts.

In addition to knowing the content of each text, you should be able to identify the themes and ideas in them. This is especially important when you are revising the poems in Section One, as themes and ideas are part of the focus of question 1. For each text you should note down what these are. When you notice the same theme occurring in more than one text, you should try to identify the writer's attitude to it. For example, Frost may have differing attitudes to the theme of work or nature in his poems and you should be prepared to write about these differing attitudes in your answer.

As you have seen, the concern of questions 1 and 2 is with the writer's or speaker's methods, which include, of course, the way in which he or she uses language to create and convey meanings and purpose. Therefore, part of your exam preparation should focus on the way in which the writers use language. For each text, you should identify what you consider are the writer's most important or significant uses of language and their effects, so that you do not have to work this out in the exam itself.

It has already been mentioned that one of the prime causes of candidates losing marks is that they sometimes choose to write on texts which are either irrelevant or inappropriate. However well you might write an answer on a particular text, if it is not one that allows you to answer the question, the examiner cannot award you any marks. It would not be fair to those other candidates who did choose appropriately. You should therefore practise choosing appropriately. Look at past papers (your teacher will have copies of them or you can find them on the AQA website) and select texts in discussion with other students or your teacher and be prepared to justify your choice of texts.

Annotation

Most of the suggestions made above are likely to involve annotating your *Anthology*. It is worth reminding you at this point what the specification says about annotation:

> The *Anthology* taken into the examination room may contain only brief marginal annotation. Such annotation should amount to no more than cross-references and/or the glossing of individual words or phrases. Highlighting and underlining is permitted. Annotations going beyond individual words or phrases, or amounting to *aides-mémoire* or notes towards the planning of essays are not permitted. Insertion of pages, loose sheets, 'post-its' or any other form of notes or additional material is not permitted.

The crucial points to note here are that you are permitted only 'brief marginal annotation', 'cross-references', 'glossing' and 'highlighting and underlining'. Therefore, the best annotations to use are *brief* notes about the themes and ideas found in a text and perhaps some highlighting of specific language features and methods, together with a brief marginal reminder of what the feature is and its importance. You may also like to devise your own colour coding as a handy guide.

We have already indicated that the examiner is interested in your own ideas and responses to the texts and that these are more important than your teacher's or the examiner's. There is a danger in having too much marginal annotation. Not only is it against the rules of the specification, but it can also be unhelpful to you.

For example, you may have made notes in the margin when you dealt with a text in class and have copied down what your teacher said. Not only will these notes not be your own ideas and responses to the text, but the lesson could have taken places months before the exam and your memory (or notes) of what was said and discussed may be patchy. If you have such notes in your *Anthology*, you may be tempted to rely on them too much in the exam. You might think that because you have these notes, they must be relevant to the question or be better than your own ideas and responses. This may not be the case. Far too frequently examiners come across answers in which the candidate has obviously cobbled together an answer from half-understood or remembered marginal annotation, which results in either an irrelevant answer or one in which the candidate is clearly not responding to the text in a personal way. So, the rules about annotation are to be followed not only because they *are* the rules, but because they are likely to lead to a much more successful answer.

Brief and focused annotation is the rule of the day.

How to ensure a successful exam answer

You have been to all the lessons, done all the work your teacher has asked of you and revised as thoroughly as possible. Now all that is left is the exam itself. You want to get the best mark possible. If you follow the tips in this section, you should be well on your way to achieving high marks.

Read the question

This may seem too obvious to mention, but there are many candidates whose answers give the impression that they have not read the question. Examiners take considerable care to ensure that the questions posed are as clear and straightforward as possible and provide a fair challenge. They do, however, expect that a candidate will answer the question that has been set. Don't be one of those candidates who go into the exam room having tried to predict what will be asked and prepared accordingly and who are then unable to answer anything other than the question they have been expecting. If your answer is not relevant to the question posed, then an examiner cannot give you many marks. The mark scheme will have been prepared in the light of these questions and it would be unfair to those candidates who do try to answer the question relevantly if irrelevant answers were rewarded.

Plan your answer

If you look around the exam room, no doubt you will see people writing answers almost as soon as they have read the question. You may be tempted to do the same to avoid wasting time. Candidates who begin writing straightaway are misguided. You need to give yourself time to *plan* and *organise* your response once you have seen the question. Examiners welcome a well-structured and organised answer, as it is the sign of a good and thoughtful candidate. You should therefore take some time to plan. This will involve selecting appropriate texts, ordering the points you are going to make and choosing evidence from the text to support these points. In this exam you have 45 minutes per question and each question requires you to write on two texts. In effect, then, you have just over 22 minutes to spend on each text. You should use about four or five of these 22 minutes to plan and order what you are going to say about each text.

Choose appropriate texts

Candidates lose more marks by choosing inappropriate texts than for almost any other reason. You can see therefore why thinking carefully about the texts you are going to explore is an essential part of planning. Don't choose texts because you have just revised them, or you think some are easier than others or you have more notes on some — choose them because they are *relevant to the question*.

Focus immediately on the question

Twenty-two minutes is not a long time to focus on a text. Therefore, you cannot afford to waste time with general introductions about, say, Frost's poetry, themes or contextual background. Examiners see this as time-wasting waffle. They want to see from your very first words that you are engaging with the question asked. Marks are not awarded for generalised introductions, so you should not spend any time on them.

Write clear and accurate English

Slips of the pen under the pressure of an exam are easily made and if there are not too many, examiners will ignore them. If, however, there is consistent mis-spelling or many unpunctuated sentences, then you will lose marks. You should ensure therefore that the points you make are expressed clearly and that there is no garbled syntax to impede an examiner's understanding of your thoughts. You would not want to spoil your good ideas about a text by not expressing them clearly. It follows from this that you should check through what you have written, not only at the end of the question, but from time to time while you are writing your answer.

Use appropriate terminology

Linked to the need for clear and accurate English is, of course, your use of appropriate terminology. Examiners like to see candidates using terminology accurately and appropriately in their answers. Remind yourself of the use of terminology by re-reading the section on p. 16.

Manage your time

Examiners expect you to write more or less the same amount on each of the four texts. You should aim therefore to spend an equal amount of time writing about each one (about 22 minutes). Do not make the mistake of thinking that if you write well and at some length and depth on one text that this will compensate for a less thorough treatment of the second text. This is never the case. There are 35 marks per question. Though there is not a rigid division of 17½ marks per text that examiners can award, they do divide the marks approximately equally between the texts. You will lose marks if you do not then divide your time equally between the two texts. Nor should you be one of those candidates who write on only one text. Examiners are allowed to award only a maximum of 18 marks in this case. Sometimes candidates who have not managed their time well find themselves rushing at the end of the exam to say everything they want to include about a text. They decide to resort to the 'note-form' approach. While this may gain a few marks, it is almost always the case that the marks gained will be fewer than if proper time management had been in place. Examiners want to read two well-planned and executed answers in continuous and accurate prose, not hastily cobbled-together notes.

Cover all bullet points

Examiners usually put in some bullet points in question 1 to guide your thinking and your answer. This is a reminder to you that you should ensure that your answer does, in fact, deal with all the bullet points. Where a question asks you to write how language helps to create and convey ideas _and_ about how a text is structured and organised, for example, then you would be foolish not to cover both aspects. Examiners can give you marks only for what you have written, not for what you might have written.

Make detailed comments

You cannot be expected to cover everything in your answer as you have only limited time. So it is important that you select carefully the features of language in a particular text that you want to discuss. These must be the significant ones in that they help to create and convey the meaning and ideas in the text. Do not attempt to write about every aspect of language as this will lead you into making a lot of superficial points. In fact, candidates who adopt this approach invariably do badly. It is much better to concentrate on a few aspects of the way in which a writer or speaker has used language and to explore these in depth showing their contribution to the overall meaning and effect of the text. Detailed exploration of a small number of significant points is preferable to a superficial skating over the surface of many. It always gains higher marks.

Provide brief exemplification

If you adopt the approach outlined in the previous section, you will automatically be using supporting evidence from the text. Once you have identified and commented on a significant aspect of language use, there is no need to provide every instance of where it occurs in the text. For instance, if you think that a writer's use of repetition is important and have therefore discussed an example or two of it in depth, there is no need for you to cite or discuss every occurrence of repetition in the text.

Avoid the 'all-purpose' answer

Examiners sometimes refer to this approach as the 'do-it-yourself' answer. This is where a candidate has not thought clearly about what the question is asking specifically and has been panicked into writing everything that he/she knows about a particular text on the grounds that, perhaps, some part of the answer must be relevant to the question. In effect, you are asking the examiner to select the relevant parts of your answer and to ignore the rest. Not surprisingly, marks for this approach are sparse. This underlines the need for you to think carefully about what the question is asking and for you to take time to plan and organise your answer.

Now it's up to you.

Questions
&
Answers

This section provides examples of the type of essays produced by candidates in the Unit 1 examination. There are three complete answers and one that includes only the candidate's response to question 1. The first is an example of an A-grade answer, the second is a good C-grade answer and the third is a D-grade response. These are followed by one essay that gained a U grade. The U-grade answer has been included to show you the dangers and traps that an unwary candidate can fall into when answering on the poetry of Robert Frost.

There are two questions on the paper: question 1 is on poems from Section One of the *Anthology*; question 2 is on the texts from Section Two of the *Anthology*. Each question is marked out of 35 marks.

It is important that you do not treat these answers as 'model' answers. They have been chosen to exemplify important points and to guide you in your preparation for your examination.

The questions that the candidates were answering are as follows:

(1) Look again at 'The Oven Bird'. By careful reference to this poem and to *one* other poem from *Section One* of the *Anthology*, show how Robert Frost writes about time and change.
   You should write about:
   • **how the language used conveys Frost's ideas**
   • **Frost's use of structure and organisation**

(2) Choose *two* texts from *Section Two* of the *Anthology* in which the writers and/or speakers show strong feelings about a town or a city.
   How do the writers and/or speakers convey these feelings?

Examiner comments

Each of the candidate answers is accompanied by examiner comments, preceded by the icon 🖉. These comments indicate what is creditable (or not) within the answer and why a particular grade would be awarded. Pay particular attention to the strengths and weaknesses identified by the examiner, and treat the examiner comments as useful advice in your preparation for the examination.

Grade-A answers

Answer to question 1

'The Oven Bird' describes the changing of the seasons throughout the year. Frost uses the first three lines of the poem to describe the Oven Bird.

e The answer begins straightaway by focusing on the question. In the very first sentence, the candidate concentrates on 'the changing of the seasons'. This is linked clearly to the theme of the question: 'time and change'. There is no generalised introductory paragraph about Frost. This is good, as time in an exam is limited.

It is, in fact, a very ordinary bird. It has no song, it merely makes a sound like 'teacher' and it makes its nest on the ground out of mud.

e This is useful contextual information about the bird. The fact that it is 'ordinary' is important in the poem. 'Everyone' has heard it. The further contextual information prevents any misunderstanding about the bird. Perhaps the candidate could briefly develop the idea of the bird as a 'teacher', as one of Frost's ideas in the poem is that the bird reminds us of (or teaches us) some important things.

The middle section of the poem (lines 4–10) is used to portray the bird's voice.

e This is not quite accurate. Rather than being a 'portrayal' of the bird's voice, Frost is writing about what the bird is telling us about the changing seasons. Of course, in reality the bird is not 'telling' us anything; Frost is using the bird's song as a reminder of an eternal truth about the changing seasons. The candidate is implicitly addressing the bullet point about 'structure and organisation'.

'He says that....' It appears that the bird simply sits by and watches the seasons pass, as he mentions 'that leaves are old'. It is as if the bird is stating that the well-nourished and beautiful leaves of a tree have succumbed to time and change.

e The candidate continues to focus on the question by writing about 'time and change'. There is a missed opportunity here to focus on the language Frost uses (bullet point 1) about the bird's song. Frost uses the word 'says' to describe this and, of course, this word usually describes human speech. Birds do not 'say' anything and perhaps the candidate could have pointed out this linkage between the bird and a human. It is a teacher.

The bird continues in his speech 'the early petal-fall is past'. This is stating that the initial quick transfer from summer to autumn has occurred and now the weather remains the same, 'overcast'.

e This is not quite right. The 'early petal-fall' marks the transition from spring to summer (line 5). It is not until line 9 that the first mention of autumn takes place. Of course, for any American reader, there will have been echoes of autumn in the word 'petal-fall', 'fall' being the American term for autumn. However, despite this mistake, the candidate has already demonstrated to the examiner that this answer is clear and focused on the question and that so far the candidate is dealing successfully with a difficult poem.

Frost uses a semicolon possibly to explain his meaning as after 'a moment overcast' he continues to say 'comes that other fall we name the fall'. The line after the semicolon is almost an attempt to justify what he's saying. The other fall is the American term for autumn, however, as the seasons are changing and things are changing from good to bad (summer to autumn).

e Here the candidate is fully back on track. He/she has picked up the reference to fall/autumn and continues to write about the changing of the seasons ('summer to autumn'). The examiner would be pleased to note that the candidate maintains concentration on the question and has not been sidetracked into any irrelevancy. The examiner would also be impressed by the close attention the candidate is paying to the language of the poem. Not many candidates would have noticed Frost's use of a semicolon (accurate terminology, too), let alone have been moved to comment on it. 'Justify' is not the right term to explain Frost's use of this punctuation mark. Perhaps the candidate could have suggested that it signals the change between the seasons of summer and autumn, but not as abruptly as a full stop would have done.

The 'fall' could be a metaphor for the fall of Man.

e The candidate notes a further meaning of the word 'fall', linking it to the theological concept of the Fall of Man, which Christians use as a metaphor for the existence of sin and evil in the world. This is a legitimate reading of the poem as, in this context, the resonances of the word 'fall' are appropriate. The candidate sensibly, however, uses the word 'could' to suggest that this is a possible rather than a certain reading.

Man started off well, but now faces more problems — global warming and loss of natural resources. The change from the good times to the times of uncertainty.

e The candidate develops this idea, giving examples of the problems that the Fall of Man has brought into the world: 'global warming and loss of natural resources'. These are contemporary concerns and not ones that Frost himself would have been familiar with, writing almost 90 years ago. This does not, however, invalidate what the candidate is saying as Frost may well be making a universal point about 'evil'. Contemporary readers of Frost's time would have been able to supply their own examples of the Fall of Man (the First World War perhaps), so it is not unacceptable for a reader in the early twenty-first century to supply more relevant illustrations. Many candidates who also saw that Frost may be making wider references to the 'fall' devoted many paragraphs to speculation on what Frost could have been referring to here, but this candidate is sensibly content to keep speculation to a minimum. The second sentence in this section of the answer continues the candidate's focus on the question, mentioning 'change'.

The third line from the end, Frost adds 'But', slowing the readers' pace, making them pause. He then goes on to say that the Oven Bird knows not to sing his song, because after autumn arrives winter.

e Again, there is a close concentration on a specific language feature: the use of the word 'But' and a sensible attempt to explain its effect. The line (line 12) that begins with 'But' is a tricky one and the candidate does not quite understand it, saying that 'the Oven Bird knows not to sing his song', but, in fact, the Oven Bird does not stop singing. One reading of the line might be that he continues to sing, but that the song (or message) is not a palatable one, dealing as it does with the change of seasons (possibly from autumn to winter, as the candidate suggests). However, the candidate would not be unduly penalised for this misreading because not only is it a difficult line in a difficult poem, but also there were far worse misreadings of the line in the answers of other candidates.

'A diminished thing' ends the poem, highlighting that possibly the best of the year has ended and the cycle will have to repeat it once more.

e Similarly, the ending of the poem with its reference to 'a diminished thing' is tricky. Many candidates overcome the difficulty simply by ignoring it. Here this candidate tackles the problem and supplies a possible reading of the phrase. He/she neatly closes this reading of the poem by a reference to 'the cycle', which again maintains focus on the question asked.

Time and change play a key role in 'Nothing Gold Can Stay'.

e The candidate's own choice of the second poem is entirely appropriate as 'time and change' do 'play a key role' in it.

The title highlights to the reader that no matter how precious something is (gold is the most precious metal) it doesn't last.

e The candidate understands the implications of the title of the poem and shows its relevance to the question being answered.

Frost uses short sentences to make his point in this poem. It is appropriate that such a short poem is being used to show how quickly something can come and go.

e Here the candidate is making a pertinent point about the language and structure of the poem. He/she is relating the brevity of the poem (only eight short lines) to the theme of the question — time and change.

'Nature's first green is gold.' The first colour that nature receives is gold. In New England, there are trees which gain gold leaves before turning to green.

e The candidate tackles head-on the puzzling ambiguity of the first line. How can 'green' be 'gold'? To answer this seeming paradox, he/she uses some contextual knowledge effectively by referring to the New England trees, which do have a golden tinge to their leaves when they first appear. This golden tinge rapidly changes to green. So Frost is describing what actually happens to these trees. Though the candidate's second sentence could have been expressed more clearly, the examiner would be pleased to note this level of understanding of this quite difficult poem.

However, it is 'her hardest hue to hold'. This use of the word 'her' makes nature a female figure, beautiful, elegant, however it is her hardest colour to keep.

e Again, the candidate pays close attention to details of the language of the poem, noting the personification of nature suggested by the use of the word 'her'.

Gold is quick to come and go, showing how the most precious things in life are the hardest to keep hold of.

e Perhaps it would be better to use the phrase 'the golden colour' rather than 'gold'.

Frost describing the early leaf being a flower again reinforces his idea of the beautiful flower appearing and then later on ('But only so an hour') quickly changing into an ordinary leaf.

e The candidate's answer follows the structure of the poem. While this is acceptable when dealing with such a short, allusive poem as this, it can be a dangerous practice for most poems. Your answer could easily become nothing more than a running commentary on the text with the points being made becoming superficial. With a long poem (as some of Frost's are in the *Anthology*) a further danger of this approach is that you might either never reach the end of the text or omit important parts of the poem. It is much better to plan your answer and ensure that you focus on the most important sections that are relevant to the question. But here, with this short poem, the approach is likely to be more fruitful.

Time and change in nature is ruthless. It can look beautiful for a while and then it changes and becomes indistinguishable to all the other trees.

e This is not a clearly expressed section, but the idea of the ruthlessness of nature is an important one that few candidates recognise.

After line 4, Frost uses a break, so he can change the feeling of the poem, 'leaf subsides to leaf' becoming indistinguishable and 'Eden sank to grief'.

e In fact, there are many 'breaks' in the poem. All the lines are end-stopped and there are five sentences in only eight lines. It is not clear what the candidate means by 'change the feeling of the poem'. This might be an important point, but the candidate does not explain what the 'feeling' is changed from and to, so it is difficult for an examiner to judge.

The use of the Garden of Eden is significant as it proves that even the perfect place can still fall into 'grief' — grief, sadness both are linked to the feeling when people, animals and nature go beyond their best.

e This is a good section, as the candidate is seeing the wider range of reference in the poem. Many candidates who answer on this poem do not deal with this line, as it is quite challenging. This candidate sees the link to the question about time and change implied in the line and makes some good points about the connection to the themes expressed earlier in the poem. Although there is no requirement to make comparisons between the two poems, a brief link to the idea of the Fall of Man referred to in the response to 'The Oven Bird' would have been appropriate and acceptable.

The final two lines are possibly the lines that sum up the poem. The image of dawn turning to day, regardless of how strong or pretty dawn is, it still has to recede and give way to 'day'.

✐ Again, the penultimate line is difficult and the candidate does not shy away from its challenge. This is to the candidate's credit. He/she also demonstrates how it links thematically to the poem with its implied reference to time and change.

The poem ends with its title, almost as if the poem is going to go round again — its time is up, so it begins again.

✐ The candidate here notes an aspect of the structure and organisation of the poem in the way that the final line repeats the title. The candidate is not content merely to identify this feature, but suggests a possible reason for it — that time and change in Frost's view are cyclical.

✐ **Overall, this is a good answer on two challenging poems. The candidate maintains a focus on the question throughout the answer and is thoughtful and responsive. He/she does not ignore the challenges posed by the poems and shows a clear understanding of them. There is equal consideration given to both; the candidate ensures that the two bullets are covered, always providing exemplification for the points made. There are some weaker sections to the answer and parts of it could have been expressed more clearly, but this does not prevent it from being a top-band response. There is, of course, much more that could have been said about either of the poems, but an examiner would not expect there to be comprehensive coverage in an answer. Time constraints prevent this. A strength of this answer is that it focuses on some of the significant aspects of the poems and deals with them in some depth. The candidate does not attempt to cover too much too superficially.**

This answer would be awarded 32 marks, a grade A.

■ ■ ■

Answer to question 2

At the beginning of chapter 5 in *Hard Times* by Charles Dickens there is a section on 'The Key Note'. The narrator seems to introduce the town as 'Coketown' to familiarise the reader with the place.

✐ This is slightly odd phrasing. 'Coketown' is the name Dickens gives to his fictional town, not to 'familiarise' the reader with the place, but because he thinks that the name encapsulates the essence of this dirty, industrial town. An examiner would surmise that this is what the candidate meant and would not penalise the candidate for this odd phrasing, but a persistent weakness of expression in an answer would result in a loss of marks. The candidate does correctly identify Dickens's intention here to 'introduce' the town to the reader.

He then takes the audience into and around Coketown, describing all they see.

During the second paragraph, Dickens uses many colour references ('red',' black', 'purple') to give the reader a sense of what people saw on a day-to-day basis.

e The focus of this question is on the methods that writers or speakers use to communicate their strong feelings about a town or city. Here the candidate, right at the start of the answer, is showing the examiner some awareness of this focus by concentrating on one of Dickens's methods — his use of colour. The candidate also suggests why Dickens does this.

It becomes apparent early on that the narrator dislikes the town for what it has become. It was a town of 'unnatural red and black', both of which are very foreboding colours and neither are welcoming. They appear to give the town the image of 'the painted face of a savage'. Cities and towns want to appear welcoming and vibrant, not painted with dark colours.

e The candidate develops this point. Sensibly, the candidate has not just mentioned Dickens's use of colours but is now going on to explore this in more detail by writing of the 'unnatural' aspect of the two colours. Again the candidate does not just identify a language feature, but explores its effect by suggesting that these are 'foreboding' and unwelcoming colours. He/she links this with the image of 'the painted face of the savage'. Note that the candidate has written approximately a third of the response to the first text, but has dealt with only the first six lines of the Dickens extract. This is quite acceptable, as the candidate is exploring the writer's methods in some detail. The passage is too long for any candidate to cover every aspect of it in the limited time available in an exam, so the candidate is sensibly being restrictive. This is a much better strategy than attempting to cover too much too superficially.

The time of the story is in the Industrial Revolution...

e This is a brief indication that the candidate is aware of the context of the passage. Much more than this would shift the focus away from what is the essence of the question.

...and it is clear that the narrator dislikes what has become of the town. He uses the images of animals to give the reader a sense of fear: 'interminable serpents of smoke' and 'elephant in a state of melancholy madness'.

e Having dealt with one of Dickens's methods, the candidate moves on to deal with another: his use of animal imagery. The candidate quotes briefly and accurately from the text and remembers to suggest an effect that this imagery has: 'to give the reader a sense of fear'.

These are not animals that would give the reader a sense of calm, they are jungle animals which do not bow to people.

e The candidate develops this point more thoroughly by showing that these are not just any animals; the 'serpents' and the 'elephant' are jungle animals, not normally found in a nineteenth-century English industrial town.

Much like the machines, they do not have feelings or a soul; they are merely there to do a task and nothing more.

e Though some may dispute the point about animals not having feelings, in this context the candidate is quite right; Dickens is more concerned with their mechanistic aspect and the candidate points this out.

The narrator seems to feel that there is no warmth or security in the town any more, the machines are working 'monotonously' — no feeling or desire, it is just repetitive and dull.

e Again, the candidate focuses in detail on a specific language feature — 'monotonously' — and shows why Dickens has chosen to use this word. There is a full exploration of its effect and this would be rewarded by the examiner.

The repeated use of the word 'same' shows how single-track-minded the town has become. It is as if the narrator doesn't feel the need for a different word to use other than 'same' because nothing ever changes.

e The candidate now turns to a further method that Dickens has used: the repetition of the word 'same'. There are many other examples of repetition in the first two paragraphs. The lexical repetition of 'like one another' or the grammatical repetition of 'it was' are just two of many. The candidate cannot comment on all of these, but the examiner will be pleased that he/she has noticed this important device and, moreover, has suggested a reason why Dickens used it: 'the narrator doesn't feel the need for a different word...because nothing ever changes'. The fact also that the candidate identifies Dickens's use of a narrator is another of the writer's methods, but the candidate does not pursue this in any further detail.

The narrator feels that due to the machines and factories, Coketown is now just a servant of 'the fine lady', simply producing products for people and yet no one wants to hear of such a place as Coketown.

e A point that puzzles many candidates is explained clearly here. The candidate understands Dickens's reference to 'the fine lady' and shows its effect.

The speaker even mentions how religion cannot penetrate the dull nature of Coketown. Dickens refers to the fact that 18 religious groups had attempted to stay in Coketown — none succeeded.

e This is not quite the point that Dickens is making. Eighteen 'religious persuasions' had built churches in Coketown but they all (bar one) look the same and none of the working classes seem to attend them. The religious groups remain, however.

The fact that God and religion cannot penetrate this lowly city is a testament to how fallen and degraded Coketown is.

e Here the candidate rectifies this slight error by correctly suggesting why Dickens had mentioned the churches and chapels. This concludes the response to the Dickens passage and, of course, the candidate has dealt with less than half the text. This does not matter at all. It demonstrates clearly to the examiner that the candidate fully understands how Dickens works and the effects created and conveyed. It is time for him/her to move on to the second text, so as to maintain a balanced answer.

Alice Foley's *Growing Up* however is in total contrast to Coketown.

e This is true to a certain extent (Foley was also writing about a Lancashire industrial town, Bolton, though set some 50 years later than Dickens's view of Coketown/ Preston), but the candidate does not need to compare or contrast the choice of texts.

Although the place where Foley lived was not a very prosperous area, no one ever felt down-hearted. The street in which I was 'nurtured' almost suggests that the street (or the people in it) looked after her. The use of the pronoun 'our' signifies that the people felt it was *their* street and no one else's. In a sense they were all in it together as one.

e Again, the candidate pays close attention to the writer's use of specific language features and comments on the effect conveyed.

The speaker accepts that they weren't of rich status but it was the same for every-body, 'all were of a ruck', again symbolising that they were all in it together and they were there for each other.

e The candidate could have commented on the fact that Foley's use of 'all were of a ruck' is colloquial and, presumably, dialectal, contributing therefore to the warm, local feeling generated by the whole passage. He/she does comment later on local language features.

Whereas in *Growing Up* everybody helps everybody else, in Coketown, there was no one.

e Again, the point about comparing and contrasting not being a requirement of this unit could be made here. However, it does show that the candidate is thinking intelligently about the chosen texts.

Again the use of the pronoun 'we' — 'washing up days we tolerated', no one was alone, everybody stuck together.

e The candidate's control of language has slipped a little here. The candidate has written a sentence without a main verb. This is a characteristic of candidates either who are running out of time or who have taken a 'feature-spotting' approach to their texts. Neither impresses an examiner.

A further example of this is the fact that if someone won money betting on the horses, then they may buy a suit and lend it to people, 'Con I borrow your John's suit'. The use of phonetic spelling shows how the narrator wants to let the reader see how things were said in Bolton. This shows confidence in the town, street and childhood.

e Here the candidate does make the point about the effect created by Foley's use of local dialect, characterised by her attempt to indicate the local accent by her use of non-standard spelling — 'con' for 'can'.

The narrator feels so passionately about her street that when things were pawned they were redeemed 'in order to maintain the dignity of our street'. The street is personal and precious.

The spirit of the street could be voiced through the 'knocker-up' who would call out the time of day and sometimes the weather. For this volunteered service he received 'four pence per week from each household'. They didn't have to pay him nor did he have to act as the knocker-up, yet he did it nonetheless. Again, Foley uses the colloquial term 'knocker-up' to almost show off her street and town. They had their own terms for particular jobs.

e There is a danger that the candidate is falling slightly into the trap of summarising the content of the text, telling the examiner here what the knocker-up's duties were. Luckily, the candidate does not do this often, but be wary of doing it in your answers. Examiners do not want to read a summary of what they themselves have already read in a text and always penalise candidates who take this path. In this answer, the candidate does make a relevant point about Foley's use of 'the colloquial term'.

This repeated use of colloquial terms and phonetic spelling implies that the narrator wants the reader to be a part of her experience and her childhood. Almost as if she enjoys telling her story to whoever is willing to listen. Along with the phonetic spelling is the bright, happy and vibrant adjectives, 'cheerful', 'loved', 'warm smell', all of these are inviting images to the reader. There are no demoralising or negative feelings portrayed in the poem. The narrator maintains a high and positive account throughout *Growing Up*.

e This is a good paragraph containing a number of relevant points about Foley's methods. The candidate mentions again her use of 'colloquial terms' and 'phonetic spelling' and her use of 'vibrant adjectives'. A minor annoyance to the examiner is the labelling of the extract from a prose memoir as a 'poem'. This is something that weaker and more casual candidates do all the time and it invariably suggests to the examiner that here is a candidate guilty of sloppy thinking. You would be well advised to avoid this practice.

e **This is a good response. There is clear, detailed and undivided focus on the question, demonstrating a good understanding of both the content and contexts of the two chosen texts. The candidate concentrates on the methods that each writer uses, supporting and developing points consistently with detailed analysis of the language of the texts. He/she does not make the mistake of trying to include too much, and explores in depth rather than skims the surface. Through the analysis of the methods used by both Dickens and Foley, the candidate demonstrates successfully how the two writers' strong feelings and attitudes towards their respective towns were created and conveyed. This answer would be awarded 34 marks, a grade A.**

Grade-C answers

Answer to question 1

'The Oven Bird' is a descriptive poem about a particular bird.

e To call 'The Oven Bird' a 'descriptive' poem is to take a somewhat limited view. There is in fact no description of the Oven Bird's appearance or even of the nest from which it takes its name. Frost concentrates on the bird's song and on the message (and its wider significance) that he purports to hear in it. All the bird is in effect doing is to sing. The poem's central concern is not with what the bird looks like but with Frost's reflections on its somewhat harsh song.

The fact that Frost describes the bird as a 'mid-wood' bird shows the reader that he has a lot of knowledge about nature and birds.

e This is a rather empty point. It is not central to the question that the examiner has posed, but is a brief general comment. The candidate is wasting time here, as he/she has not yet earnt any marks.

The main theme that becomes clear in this poem is the changing of seasons.

e This is the final sentence of the three-sentence first paragraph. None of the three are linked, but each is making a separate point: the first about description, the second about Frost's knowledge of nature and this one about the theme of the poem. The candidate should ensure that the paragraph as a whole is coherent, focusing on just one aspect. In this case, the candidate should begin by talking about the theme of the poem as the he/she sees it: 'the changing of the seasons'. This would have clearly focused on the question right from the start.

There is a suggestion that Frost is talking about spring through his poetry, through the pragmatics of the poem 'Mid-summer is to spring as one to ten', here Frost is emphasising that spring is better than mid-summer. He sees the changes as being more positive, which happens through time.

e There are a number of weaknesses in this paragraph. The first sentence is vague with a reference to 'a suggestion'. Frost does refer to 'spring' as the quotation indicates; it is not merely a suggestion. The difficulty for the candidate is that he/she is not sure what Frost means by the line quoted. The candidate also uses the word 'pragmatics'. This is a difficult concept and is one best avoided unless you are absolutely certain that you are using it correctly. Here it seems to be used in the sense of 'hidden meaning'. It would be better to continue to write about the theme referred to at the end of the first paragraph, rather than introduce a term which is used rather vaguely. Examiners do not like references to the 'hidden meaning' of a poem, as they feel that it reduces poetry to the level of a crossword puzzle. It would be better to refer to the idea of ambiguity or to suggest that some poems may allow a variety of readings. The candidate goes on to say that 'Frost is emphasising that spring is better than mid-summer'. It is more that Frost is observing, albeit rather mathematically, a fact of the natural cycle of the seasons. Summer leaves are older than springtime ones and most of the spring blossom has in fact fallen by summer. There are, in comparison, only a few blossoms left on a tree by midsummer. It is not a question of being 'better' or seeing the changes as being 'positive'. If anything, the 'petal-fall' is a 'diminish(ing) thing'. However, the candidate would be credited by the examiner for referring to the focus of the question — time and change.

He uses the semantic field of seasons to suggest change in time.

e It is not really a 'suggestion'. Frost is indeed concerned with the change of the seasons.

The fact that in nature things die, 'early petal-fall is past', the trees have lost their petals. However, on a deeper metaphorical level Frost could be relating this to the death of human life.

e The candidate is right to suggest that this is an allusive poem, as with the reference to 'the death of human life'. This is a possible reading of the poem, though somewhat overstated. However, to make this suggestion more convincing for the examiner, the candidate ought to provide more supportive evidence for this view. As it is, the statement appears out of nowhere and is proclaimed too baldly.

In detail Frost uses the bird to emphasise change and time. The fact that the bird brings the tree to life at the beginning of the poem because of it being 'a singer everyone has heard...who makes the solid tree trunks sound again', seeing the bird a positive creature in nature.

e There is focus on the question here with the reference to 'change and time' and the candidate demonstrates understanding of the opening of the poem. The point about the Oven Bird being seen as 'a positive creature in nature' is a sensible one, though the syntax used gives the feel of the idea merely being tacked on to the end of the sentence. Clarity of expression is not all it could be here. There is also a sense of not thoroughly planning the answer as the candidate has now returned to the start of the poem in the middle of the essay.

Then towards the end of the poem 'The bird would cease and be as other birds', not sing, just like the other birds, because of the change in seasons, as it has been suggested that it is now autumn in this section of the poem.

e The candidate is making a contrast between the bird in summer and in autumn. This is a sensible thing to do. He/she does not appear to understand the point that Frost is making about the Oven Bird here. To be fair to the candidate, they are difficult lines to understand, but Frost's point is that the Oven Bird is not like the other birds. The other birds do stop singing and this is what the Oven Bird himself would like to do, but feels he must continue to sing in autumn, though the song he sings (or lesson he teaches or question he asks) is not a welcome one.

Through the language that Frost has used, 'And comes that other fall we name the fall', the syntax and repetition emphasise the change in seasons here.

> *e* Here the candidate is attempting to make a point about the effect of language, but it remains an assertion rather than a convincing proof. An examiner would ask the question of this statement: 'Exactly what is it about Frost's use of syntax and his use of repetition that emphasises the change in seasons?' All that the candidate does is to state it as a fact rather than to demonstrate the validity of this assertion.

Frost does not quite make the semantics clear in this poem. It leaves the audience thinking, is change a positive or negative thing? However, he could be linking this to death on a deeper level of semantics. Should we celebrate or mourn? The idea of the bird changing throughout this poem could parallel the poet.

> *e* The candidate packs a lot into this final paragraph on 'The Oven Bird', none of which is really satisfactory. The candidate is right to note that Frost ends the poem on an enigmatic question, but is rather woolly when accusing Frost of not writing clearly. Examiners do not like it when candidates seek to excuse their own difficulties of understanding by trying to blame the poet for not writing clearly, as this candidate appears to do here. It is not clear what is meant by 'he could be linking this to death on a deeper level of semantics'. The difficulty this candidate (and many others) has with this poem is that Frost is not writing a descriptive poem about a bird, but is using the bird and its song to represent significant issues about existence. The final sentence about the 'bird changing' 'parallel(ing) the poet' is a legitimate one (after all, Frost has written of the Oven Bird as a 'singer', a word often used for poets), but here it seems more of an afterthought, rather than a developed idea.

In 'The Need of Being Versed in Country Things', Frost has structured the poem into four stanzas.

> *e* This is an entirely appropriate choice of poem to enable the candidate to answer the question, but this sentence will not impress the examiner at all. The poem has six, not four, stanzas. In an exam in which you have the poem in front of you, this is an inexcusable error.

Through the stanzas, he describes a different time (in each stanza).

> *e* Again, a close reading of the poem that you have in front of you would reveal that this is not the case. For example, even in the first stanza, there are two times referred to — the time of the fire and the 'now', the aftermath of the fire.

This represents how things have changed in this situation, and structuring it in four stanzas makes it clearer for the reader.

> *e* The candidate is right to claim that the poem is about change, but compounds the earlier error by continuing to write of four stanzas.

The structure is also made clear by the techniques used to shape the semantics of the poem.

📝 Again, this is an unclear statement. Just what does 'shape the semantics' mean?

As in stanza one, we know straightaway that Frost is talking about the past, 'The house *had* gone'. This technique is simple but effective.

📝 Here the candidate does show understanding. There is a focus on a central issue both of the poem and of the question: 'time and change'.

He also uses a simile in the first stanza, 'like a pistil after the petals go', suggesting that something has gone. In this case the house has burnt down, 'the midnight sky a sunset glow', suggesting that things are going to change.

📝 It is not quite the case that 'things are going to change'; they *have* changed — the house, apart from the chimney, has been burnt down.

In the poem there is a reference to destiny, 'Had it been the will of the wind', saying that things change for a reason. (One of Frost's ideas about change portrayed.) In the third stanza, Frost describes scenes from the past (before this happened), emphasising how things would have been before but through time they have changed. The idea of 'teams' of horses that would have 'brush(ed) the mow with the summer load'. Very descriptive stanza of a busy, everyday scene of farm work.

📝 There is a sense that the candidate has shifted into running commentary mode now, making points but not developing them. For instance, he/she merely states that one of Frost's ideas about change is that 'things change for a reason' and is content to leave it at that. The final sentence of this paragraph is note-like.

There is then a change in attention in the poem. He sees the negative out of what has happened but realises there is positive. He uses another element, 'birds that came to it through the air', as no one can access it through the road any more. In the dead building there is still the life of the birds. The building is still accommodating life, so therefore in this poem Frost sees the changes as being positive. He is being hopeful, the fact that the birds are not sad because they have somewhere to live, 'For them there was really nothing sad'. Out of death and change and through time comes regeneration. The semantic field of death and regeneration suggests his thoughts of time and change to see it positively.

📝 The candidate makes some useful observations in this section. He/she notes that 'in the dead building' there is still 'the life of the birds' and comments that, for Frost, this is a 'positive' sign. Even in the midst of death, there is the possibility of life, as both the lilac and the elm are sprouting new leaves and the birds can find somewhere to perch and nest. The candidate explores these ideas in detail and supports the argument with evidence from the text. This, in fact, is the strongest part of this response to the poem. There is, however, a weakness in that the candidate chooses to ignore the final two lines. Here Frost seems to be suggesting that only those who are well 'versed in country things' realise that the birds (a phoebe is a flycatcher) are not actually sad or weeping; they are just behaving naturally. It is sentimental to believe otherwise. The candidate does not consider the conclusion of the poem and this weakens an otherwise good section of this answer.

Accepting that things in nature change so therefore things in life change too. He uses nature to reflect his thoughts.

e This is a flat conclusion to the answer.

e **Overall, the candidate addresses the question in this answer, but does not demonstrate a secure understanding of either poem. There are some parts where the candidate clearly demonstrates ability and potential (the section at the end of the account of the second poem, for example), but there are too many examples of sloppy reading or misunderstanding. Some of the points made remain underdeveloped. The answer would be awarded 16 marks.**

■ ■ ■

Answer to question 2

In 'The Key Note' Dickens portrays his feelings about the town that he is describing very strongly. He conveys his feelings through his language and techniques that he uses.

e There is little here that an examiner can reward. The first sentence indicates only that the candidate has chosen to write about the Dickens extract (an appropriate choice of text); the second is self-evident. What else could Dickens have used other than 'language and techniques'?

Dickens constantly uses negative, harsh adjectives to describe the town, 'unnatural'.

e Again, this is true — but it remains an undeveloped statement.

He uses a lot of animal imagery, showing a metaphorical level. He uses metaphors such as 'serpents of smoke', likening the smoke to serpents portrays it as negative.

e The candidate is identifying a particular method that Dickens uses to convey his feelings about Coketown and uses appropriate terminology, but the comment that this metaphorical use of language is 'negative', while true, is limited.

Through his detailed description he uses extended metaphors. Images such as the jungle. The serpents and the 'elephant. Monotonously...melancholy madness' alliteration emphasising the movement of the elephant.

e This has the feel of feature-spotting. Dickens *does* use 'extended metaphors' of animals and the jungle, but all that the candidate is doing here is identifying the images of the 'serpents and the elephant'. There is no attempt to explore the reasons behind Dickens's choice of imagery. The assertion that the alliteration emphasises the 'movement of the elephant' is unconvincing. Examiners invariably treat with suspicion any claims for the reasons behind a writer's use of features such as alliteration, assonance and enjambement. They are often flights of fancy. You should make such claims with caution. None of the final three sentences of this section contains a main verb. This reinforces the impression of feature-spotting; it is almost as if the candidate were pressed for time and reduced to writing in notes at this point.

The 'savage', all of these creatures link to negative jungle imagery. The elephant itself can link to the town, the fact that it is so big and loud relates to the town.

> *e* There is an attempt here to exemplify the nature of the extended image with the reference to the 'savage' and this would gain some credit. However, the claim that the 'elephant' 'can link to the town' is dubious and unsubstantiated.

The 'smoke' being negative, linking it to serpents, the smoke is almost appearing to strangle the buildings, just like the serpents would do in the jungle. It is an extended metaphor.

> *e* The candidate continues the exploration of the extended metaphor. The examiner would be pleased to see this detailed consideration of one of Dickens's techniques in the extract and would reward this attempt at exploring the effect created. This explanation is more convincing than the previous one.

Also, the imagery of hell, 'a black canal', extremely negative showing how Dickens feels.

> *e* It is not clear from what the candidate writes here how 'a black canal' can conjure up an image of 'hell' — negativity, perhaps, but hell?

Dickens describes the town using dull colours, reflecting how he thinks the people are in the town. The dull colours such as 'unnatural red', 'black' reflects how dull the people's lives are in the town.

> *e* The candidate moves on to another of Dickens's techniques. It is right to note his use of 'red' and 'black', but it is not really the dullness that Dickens is referring to, but rather the unnaturalness and savagery. The candidate omits his description of the river as 'purple', which is perhaps the most unnatural aspect of colour in the town. It would have been better to use the 'black and white' (line 30) as evidence of dullness and strictness. The candidate does, however, gain some credit for the observation that Dickens is using colour to convey his 'strong feelings' about Coketown.

People's attitudes are straightforward, there is no room for imagination. The grammar that Dickens uses, list of three and repetition 'fact, fact, fact' emphasises that they live dull, boring lives. Also 'fact' being a monosyllabic word, a harsh sounding word. It is emphatic, reflects the attitudes of the people and the environment.

> *e* This is a better paragraph. The candidate identifies correctly further techniques and the suggestions made about the effect of these techniques are sensible.

Dickens uses negative names 'M'Choakumchild' using the semantic field of names from the town to describe its pollution. The fact that pollution can choke people.

> *e* The candidate is right here to identify Dickens's use of names to indicate his feelings and the examiner would credit the identification of the negative name 'M'Choakumchild'. However, he/she is not right in linking the name to the environmental pollution in Coketown alluded to in the extract; the name is used by Dickens to indicate the way

that the school system stifles a child's creativity and imagination. The candidate would not be expected to know this, as this knowledge can come only from a reading of other parts of the novel, so, in this case, an examiner would be happy to reward this reading linking the name to pollution (which, in a sense, it is).

The random number of 'eighteen' that Dickens states is a random number making the extract from the prose fiction seem more realistic and more believable for the reader.

e There is no evidence supplied for this statement and little credit can be given for it.

There is contrast in the extract, the fact that the people live dull lives and yet they produce beautiful things, 'gold'.

e A potentially good point which the candidate has, unfortunately, left undeveloped.

The tone throughout is extremely negative. Detailed descriptions which are negative convey how Dickens feels.

e These two sentences add nothing to what the candidate has already said and could well have been omitted. The negativity towards Coketown felt by Dickens has been mentioned a number of times.

He uses religious imagery as well, another contrast, 'pious', holy and religious, a good religion. 'Religious persuasion' being types of churches showing that the town is religious but at the same time so negative due to pollution and industrialisation is a bad development because of how it affects particular towns.

e Again, the point that Dickens is making negative comments about religion in Coketown is a potentially good one. However, the candidate does not make the most of it. He/she defines 'pious' and, to some extent, 'religious persuasion' but follows these definitions with some muddled thinking and unclear expression. There is a sense that the candidate is trying to show that Dickens is linking religious belief, industrialisation and pollution but does not succeed in making these thoughts lucid.

A very effective piece of writing.

e This is a somewhat limp conclusion to the account of the extract, which feels rather like a teacher's comment at the end of a student's essay.

Growing Up is completely different. Foley uses her memories to describe her town seeing it as a positive aspect and not mentioning many negatives. The genre is an autobiography, which is fictionalised. It is set in Bolton 1891–1973.

e The candidate begins the account of *Growing Up* (an appropriate text for this question) by indicating correctly its positive view of the town compared with Dickens's negative one. He/she is not quite accurate in identifying its genre as fictionalised autobiography; it is more of a memoir of childhood and there is no real indication that it is at all fictionalised. Nor is it set in Bolton 1891–1973; 1891 is the year of Alice Foley's birth and 1973 was the date of publication of the memoir.

Throughout the piece there is a strong sense of community, 'Our Street'. The use of capitals symbolises how they knew it as 'their' street (their own close community).

e This is a brief but appropriate identification of one of the writer's methods by which she conveys her strong, positive feelings about her hometown.

She uses positive language throughout to convey her feelings about the town.

e This assertion requires considerable amplification and exemplification.

Her language shows that she was proud to live there even though they were poor. They worked together and helped one another.

e The same applies to this point.

When Foley describes the characters in the piece, she focuses on individual people and the descriptions are very detailed, showing the reader how close the community was. She uses senses to describe them effectively. Smell, 'hot pea man', and sound using their voices as part of the dialect, the sound of the 'children calling'.

e The candidate identifies successfully one of Alice Foley's main methods here — her detailed focus on and description of individuals in the small community of her street. He/she also points out the writer's use of sensory impressions to bring these people to life, but does not push these responses far enough. The examples cited of smell and sound, while correct, have the feel of being hastily written, and are little distant from notes.

The structure and layout of the piece links to the structure of the actual street. Describing next door at first and then continuing to describe the rest of the place.

e Again, this is a good point rendered somewhat less effective by merely being mentioned and then swiftly abandoned. The pressure of time in the exam may well have been an explanation for this. However, the examiner would give some reward for what the candidate has written because it demonstrates that he/she is focusing on the writer's methods and not merely summarising the content of the piece, as many students do.

The dialect in the piece is really effective, the phonetic spelling, accent makes the street come alive for the reader and makes us realise how positive the community was. It also makes the characters appear more realistic, 'Con I borrow your John's suit? aa reet'.

e Another of the writer's methods is identified clearly here and its effect and success are commented on.

She describes it as 'nurturing', emphasising the love/care of being brought up in such a nice community.

e The sense of time running out is apparent here. The point, again, is a valid one but it would have been better linked to the point made earlier about 'Our Street'. The examiner might suspect that the candidate has not had time to plan this answer thoroughly, but will have noted, nevertheless, the appropriateness of the observation.

Foley uses standard English, even though she states that her mum could not read or write. This shows she was well educated, unlike a lot of others.

e This may well be so, but it is not relevant to the question.

Even though conditions were poor, Foley describes it positively as this is how she remembers it 'when the evenings grew too dark for further play and it was still too early to go indoors'. This shows the poor conditions. The fact that the parents did not want the children in the house because it was just too cramped. 'Strap' basis, almost like a 'tab', this tells the reader that the people who lived on Foley's street trusted one another. They relied on trust, again another positive thought.

e This is not really analysis of Foley's methods; it remains descriptive of what went on in the Bolton street of her childhood. Some focus is being lost here.

Foley's feelings are very positive throughout, a close community, trustworthy and loving. Her language which she uses is positive, the way she describes people and places is positive. It is very personal, as the whole piece is her own personal past memories. Her feelings towards growing up in her town are very positive, due to the surroundings and the loving people which she describes etc.

e The candidate writes a repetitive final paragraph (four mentions of 'positive') which does not add much to what has already been said. The examiner would not be able to give any marks for such a conclusion.

e This is an answer in which there is a balance of strengths and weaknesses. The candidate maintains focus on the question to a large extent, though this focus becomes somewhat blurred towards the end of the essay, and shows understanding of both the content and the contexts of the chosen texts. He/she discusses in some detail both Dickens's and Foley's use of language, but, again towards the end of the response to each text, these points become a little lightweight. There is a generally accurate use of terminology throughout the answer. This answer would be awarded 22 marks. The total mark for the two questions is 38, which would gain a grade C.

Grade-D answers

Answer to question 1

I am going to look at how Frost writes about time and change in both poems 'The Oven Bird' and 'Nothing Gold Can Stay'.

e 'Nothing Gold Can Stay' is a good choice. It is clearly relevant to the question and is short enough to be manageable in the time available.

First in 'The Oven Bird' uses a metaphor to help bring spring forth. 'Who makes the solid tree trunks sound again.' This makes the reader think that as the bird starts to sing, spring is becoming closer.

e There are two matters here that would concern an examiner. First, the candidate's quality of written communication is less than admirable and, second, there is a serious misreading of the poem. The Oven Bird is, as line 2 of the poem makes clear, 'a mid-summer and a mid-wood bird', so it is sloppy of the candidate to refer to the approach of *spring* as the bird begins to sing. An examiner would not be impressed by such careless misreading. The best that can be said here is that the candidate recognises the theme of change as important in the poem.

He uses the word 'diminished' on the last line of the poem which, in context to the previous line, sounds like the world has changed and that it isn't as good as what it used to be.

e The candidate is correct to identify 'diminished' as an important word in the poem. It does indeed signal change — a change that Frost appears to regret. However, much has been omitted — eleven lines, in fact. The candidate moves from a consideration of line 3 in his/her first paragraph to writing about the last line of the sonnet — hardly a thorough examination of the whole poem. An examiner would expect a more systematic treatment of the poem than is presented in this answer.

This is also shown in 'Nothing Gold Can Stay' when it says 'Nothing gold can stay'. This is the last line of the poem and it also shows dimunition because the purity of the first shoots of nature in spring cannot last forever.

e Here the candidate links the poems (though there is no need to) by comparing ideas about diminution (not 'dimunition' as the candidate writes) and change by focusing on the last line of the poem. It is a difficult line, which repeats the title of the poem, but he/she has made a sensible attempt at explaining what it means by suggesting that Frost is using gold as a symbol of purity that is quickly tarnished. The examiner would credit this idea.

He uses references to sins and the Garden of Eden in both poems.

e Again, this line links ideas found in the poems.

For example, in 'Nothing Gold Can Stay', it says 'So Eden sank to grief'. This is the original sin which Adam and Eve made. Since that sin nothing will ever be as good as it used to be and shows that time has influences on it.

e This is a sensible, if poorly expressed point. The candidate tries to focus on the idea of time and change. Note, however, that he/she does not refer specifically to the link between purity and Eden, which is clearly present in the poem. A better answer would have referred to the previous paragraph by pointing out the purity of gold and the purity of Adam and Eve before Eve ate the apple. However, credit would still be given for the awareness that the candidate does show.

Also in 'The Oven Bird' it says 'And comes that other fall we call fall'.

e This is another example of sloppy reading. The line should read 'And comes that other fall we name the fall'. There is no excuse for such misquotation, as you have the text with you in the examination.

This refers to the beginning of sin as well. Ever since the sin the world has been fading away, again using dimunition.

e This is a potentially good point about the effects of the Fall of Man, but the candidate does not expand on it. An examiner would know what the candidate is trying to say here, but cannot do the work for him/her. The point needs to be clearly explained to earn credit.

'The Oven Bird' also has references to urbanisation. This is an increasing thing over the past few decades. The poem says 'He says the highway dust is over all'. Meaning that he is criticising the progress of building towns and cities, which when built, destroy the countryside.

e This is a possible reading of the line about the 'highway dust', but, again, the examiner has to do the work for the candidate, who does not explain the point clearly. The point probably being made here is that Frost could be suggesting that one of the consequences of human sin and selfishness (referred to in the 'fall') is the increasing destruction of the countryside through urbanisation and industrialisation, which he represents as 'the highway dust [being] over all'. But the candidate does not spell this out, as better students would. Note, too, that apart from the opening paragraph, there has been little mention of 'The Oven Bird'.

'Nothing Gold Can Stay' uses rhyming couplets throughout the poem, which puts an emphasis on moving and flowing.

e Here the candidate comments on the structure of the poem but does not refer to this aspect of 'The Oven Bird'. Examiners tend to view with suspicion any reference to 'flowing' in a poem, not only because it is a vapid and meaningless concept but also because many (usually weaker) candidates write 'It makes the poem flow better', where 'It' could be any feature that the candidate chooses at random. You would be well advised never to mention 'flowing' in any of your answers, because for examiners it always signals a weak candidate who has nothing to say.

This could represent the passing of time.

> Nature's first green is *gold*,
> Her hardest hue to *hold*.

This quote could also mean that Nature's first green is the most valuable and trying to keep hold of it for long is hard to do.

e No real point is being made here about Frost's use of rhyming couplets, but there is a good reading of the meaning of the couplet, which would earn some credit. Note, however, as for 'The Oven Bird', the candidate does not write about other important parts of this poem, so he/she is not being systematic.

In 'The Oven Bird' there is an irregular rhyme scheme, but it still keeps a tempo and again could mean the passing of time.

e This is as meaningless as the earlier remark about 'flowing'. How does the 'irregular rhyme scheme keep a tempo'? What tempo? What is the evidence for such a remark? No credit would be given here.

The last line of this poem says 'Is what to make of a diminished thing'. This may give the impression of war because the summer is gradually killing spring.

e The candidate has already referred to the last line of the poem and should have planned his/her answer better. The point about 'war' is dubious. No convincing evidence for this reading is offered and it may come from some biographical information about Frost that the candidate was given.

The caesurer [**spelling!**] after 'loud' in the second line of 'The Oven Bird' creates an emphasis on the bird which could be ambiguous. Meaning the bird could just be innocent or it could be Frost and him expressing his feelings.

e This point appears to be an afterthought. Why return to line 2 at the end of the answer? The point is neither explored nor convincing and is a poor conclusion to the answer.

e **Overall, this is an unsatisfactory answer. The candidate does make some good points that indicate some understanding of the poem, but too many points are asserted and not proven. He/she pays almost no attention to the second bullet point in the question on structure and organisation. There is little reference to the Oven Bird as a bird and large parts of both poems remain untouched. Credit would be given for the quality of understanding shown at times, but this would not be enough to put the answer into the 18–23 mark band. A mark of 13 would be awarded.**

■ ■ ■

Answer to question 2

I am going to use 'London Z to A' and *Growing Up* to show how writers show strong feelings about a town or city.

 This is a sensible choice of texts.

First in 'London Z to A', the writer, U. A. Fanthorpe, uses a play on words in the title of the text. This could be emplying negativity in London.

 The candidate notes the playfulness of the poem's title, but he/she is unable to see that what Fanthorpe is doing by choosing this title is looking back from the present (Z) into London's history (A). The candidate's explanation is thin and misspelled.

In the first line nature is linked to buildings when it says 'Her buildings come and go like leaves'.

 The candidate makes the link between nature and London's buildings and, in the next two sentences, develops this sensibly by reference to change and destruction.

This shows that buildings are always changing and nothing is left as it was. This may mean destroying historical buildings with famous pasts.

Straightaway you can see that the writer is trying to impose a negative view on London and the progress it is making in urbanisation.

 This sentence is linked in content to the previous ones and therefore does not need a separate paragraph. Single-sentence paragraphs are often indicative of a less confident candidate.

On the other hand, in *Growing Up*, the writer is trying to show a simplistic yet pleasant life in Lancashire. This is created by using different techniques such as parallelism and by using lots of adjectives.

 The focus on writers' methods as required by the question is clear here.

Parallelism is shown at the beginning when it says 'Washing days we tolerated, with wet clothes drying on a "maiden" obscuring the fire until evening; baking days we loved, with the warm smell of new crumbly loaves'. This helps the writer show the flow of their happy lives and helps to explain their daily routines, for example 'washing days'.

 The candidate exemplifies the parallelism mentioned in the previous paragraph but does not analyse what the parallelism consists of. It is not enough merely to quote — the quotations need to be *analysed*. Note, also, yet another mention of 'flow'.

In 'London Z to A' an extended metaphor is used throughout, being 'Her'. This personifies the buildings and makes them seem like humans, as they are the ones who always make the changes which occur.

 For a metaphor to be 'extended', it needs to go beyond one single use. The candidate is right to note that Fanthorpe personifies London through the use of 'her', but this is the only occurrence of the personification.

This text also shows the growing of different cultures: 'Ziggurats bud'. Many years ago there weren't any people from different backgrounds.

e This is another illustration of an undeveloped point, where the examiner is expected to supply what is probably in the candidate's mind but is not expressed in the answer. 'Ziggurats' is an unfamiliar and non-English word, but its implications are not discussed. The candidate could have referred profitably first to the shape of a ziggurat and second to its religious significance. Nor does he/she explore a second incidence of the nature metaphor in 'bud'.

In the third stanza of 'London Z to A', it says 'In the marble city only the barbarous street names last'. This could mean that the sacred parts are kept as memories of what was once actually there. The word 'barbarous' is quite a strong word and this could show that the writer is not happy that all there is left of a landmark is the street name.

e There is some understanding here about the rapid nature of change in contemporary London, which results in the street names being the only reminder of the past, but the understanding is not clear. The candidate is right to draw attention to 'barbarous', but he/she needs to explore the significance of the word more fully. Why does the author choose a word that has connections with barbarians? It is not enough to say that it is 'quite a strong word'.

There is the use of a lot of adjectives in *Growing Up* when the writer describes the man who lives in the bottom of the row: 'a small, sandy-haired man with a fat wife'. This gives a clear image of the locals and that everybody knows each other, maybe living in a friendly neighbourhood.

e Here the candidate returns to the second text and gives examples of the second method that he/she says Foley uses — adjectives. It might have been better to deal with one text completely before writing about the second. This would have made organising the answer easier. However, if you make valid points, then the examiner will credit them wherever they occur in the answer.

The text is written in first-person narrator with an autobiographical feel, e.g. 'I was'.

e This is another point about the writer's methods, showing focus on the question.

This gives the impression that she lived there and understands how nice it was having specific routines for each day.

e The point about neighbourliness and routine is made a number of times in this answer. It is sufficient to make a point only once. Repetition wastes time that could be spent more profitably on developing your answer. An examiner will credit a point only once, no matter how many times it is made.

The writer also uses colloquialism, which is when they use regional or local dialect: for example 'Eh wha'. When this is used it gives a feel of how the place actually was and everybody understood each other.

e This is another valid point about method. It is exemplified and its effect is evaluated, as required.

To show that they had happy simplistic lives, the writer explains the man who lived next door to the 'knocker-up' and his daily routine 'each evening after tea he released the birds from their cotes'. This shows people were happy with what they were used to and there was no need to change how they lived and the things around them.

e This is repetition about routine and neighbourliness.

In contrast to this, 'London Z to A' says 'Down remembered gone roads' meaning it was no longer there and all that was left was the memories they kept. Also the poem says 'cockney faces blossom in witty brittle facades', showing that the people who live there put happy faces on, but really inside them they know they don't like where they live or the people around them.

e The candidate attempts to make a comparison between the happy inhabitants of Bolton and the unhappy Cockneys of London. Remember that comparison is not required and note, also, that Fanthorpe does not say or imply that the Cockneys were unhappy — superficial and comic, maybe, but not unhappy. The candidate fails also to point out a real incidence of an extended metaphor: 'blossom' links with 'leaves', 'bud', 'suckers' and 'pruning' used earlier in the poem.

The only parts of nature which are left around the people who live in London are the names of the pubs, such as:

> But the corner pubs
> Honour forgotten generals, dispossessed peers,
> A stag, a tree.

There is no more nature left around London and the writer feels strongly about this and wishes things could change.

e The candidate is correct to point out that London's past is remembered only in the names of the pubs, but it is not just nature that is commemorated in these names: generals and peers have also given their names to the pubs.

Overall this poem shows that the culture of the suberbs [**spelling!**] of London have slowly diminished and has changed to just football and drinking.

e Where does the reference to 'football' come from? Fanthorpe does not mention it in the poem.

In *Growing Up* it is completely different and the writer tries to show strong feelings of happiness and that their culture has stayed. This is shown by the routines of the locals and the way they live their lives in each other's pockets.

e Routine and neighbourliness get their final mention.

e **The candidate does not demonstrate a clear understanding of 'London Z to A', but he/she makes some points that an examiner can reward. There is a better (if repetitive) response to *Growing Up*, because there is a clearer focus on Foley's methods, which is what the question asked for. This is a stronger answer than the response to question 1 and would be awarded 17 marks.**

Grade-U answer

Answer to question 1

In 'Oven Bird' and 'Out, Out —' Robert Frost writes about change and time.

e The candidate's choice of text to complement 'The Oven Bird' ('Out, Out —') is unexpected but, at this point, the examiner would give the candidate any benefit of doubt.

In 'The Oven Bird' the literal meaning of change is the bird who sang differently to all the other birds but now has to change and sing along with all the other birds.

e This is muddled and incorrect. The bird is not the 'literal meaning of change' (muddled) and it does not sing along with the other birds (incorrect). This is not a promising start.

The bird is a 'diminished thing', and as it feels diminished believes it has to be like the others to be able to carry on.

e Again, this is a sloppy reading. There is a grain of truth in what the candidate writes, but there is little understanding on display. The main point that is worth noting here is that this is the end of the candidate's account of the 'literal' meaning of the poem. From now on the candidate moves into trying to link the bird, a singer, and Frost, the poet. Too many candidates do this. It is true that this poem (and many others of Frost's in the *Anthology*) is allusive and may well have many levels of meaning, but this candidate has not even tried to explore what might be called the 'surface' meaning. He/she has dived almost straight into the muddy waters of allusion, symbolism and biography and has become stuck. This candidate would have done much better to have attempted to tease out exactly what it is that Frost is saying about the Oven Bird as a bird and the changing cycle of the seasons rather than getting so bogged down. All candidates should establish clearly what Frost is saying in his poems before moving off into these uncharted waters. Indeed, it is possible to score high marks (as we have already seen) by ignoring these tricky areas altogether.

Metaphorically this is really about Robert Frost, just like the bird is well known for singing he is a well known poet that feels he can't keep up with modern day poets and so his writing is diminishing and feels he needs to move on. His poetry is classic but feels its not what it used to be and doubts himself on whether like the bird he should change and 'cease to be as other birds'.

e The candidate has left the poem behind now and is bringing into the answer some half-understood ideas about Frost's biography as a poet. Where is the evidence in the poem for what the candidate is saying? And, just as importantly, where is the relevance to the question?

This metaphoric view of Frost's diminishing hand can also be found in 'Out, Out —'.

e Having been convinced that 'The Oven Bird' is solely about Frost's response to his supposed diminishing powers as a poet, the candidate now attempts to transfer this idea to the choice of the poem 'Out, Out —'. This is such an odd reading of the poem that it seems almost doomed to failure.

The literal meaning is a description of a boy or young man who's sawing in the backyard, he's tired of sawing and can't wait to finish. The boy ends up sawing his hand off when called in for supper. The doctor is called but 'Little — less — nothing!' The exclamative sentences writes how the boy is dead.

✒ This section is a brief, yet accurate, account of what occurs in 'Out, Out —'. This ought to be enough to warn the candidate, had he/she not been so enamoured of the idea that Frost is writing about himself as a poet, that this choice of poem is not really one that is suitable to answer a question about time and change. The only way to make this choice of poem relevant would be to write of the change that occurred in the boy's life (he died), but the main focus of the poem is on the reaction of everyone else to the boy's accidental death. The candidate has made this answer more difficult (a) by his/her choice of poem and (b) by his/her treatment of it.

Metaphorically the poem shows Frost as the young man, the saw is personified to be his writing and the cutting of the hand is the symbol of something changing and ending.

✒ There is no evidence provided by the candidate for such an odd reading of the poem.

Frost doesn't want his writing to end or change, 'Don't let him cut my hand off', the loss of the hand symbolises the loss of great writing over time and how he doesn't want to change but soon there will be nothing he can do to stop it.

✒ Nor is any evidence presented here.

In 'The Oven Bird' Frost's language helps us see his change taking place and how time is leaving him, 'Mid-summer is to spring as one to ten'. This quote shows two things that are so far away from each other just like the scale and time of life — how things can change really fast without us realising.

✒ The candidate returns to 'The Oven Bird'. It is a matter of choice how you structure your answer. You can choose to deal with one text at a time or move between the two. Examiners have no preference. You should follow whichever method you feel comfortable with. Here the candidate demonstrates a lack of understanding of the line quoted from the poem.

The quote continues 'pear and cherry blossom…sunny days a moment overcast…comes the other fall…'. It states how the summer is coming to end compared to Frost's writing coming to an end. Another year has gone for summer and for Frost, he's older and changed.

✒ There is a little for an examiner to credit here. The candidate shows understanding that Frost is dealing with the changing seasons, but perversely persists in this unprofitable interpretation of the bird as the poet. The use of quotation is poor and you should avoid this practice. First, it is too long (the candidate quotes three lines of the poem and makes one simple observation about them) and, second, he/she should not be using suspension dots. The best type of quotation to use in an essay is a short one that can be incorporated into the syntax of your sentence, so that the flow of your thought is not interrupted.

This can be compared with 'Out, Out —'s view of Frost not wanting to change and how he still sees himself as a child even though time has left him. 'The life from...old enough to know...child at heart...All spoiled.'

e Again, this is a poor use of quotation and a wrong reading of the poem. It is, in fact, a misquotation.

Frost sees himself still as a child not wanting time or writing to diminish. The saw is personified as the end. The inner conflict. The quote I have just used, in the poem has dashes at the end of the lines, to emphaises his need but remorse to change. The alliteration on 'big boy' emphaises how time has left him and he needs to leave what he use to be and grow with the times.

e The candidate makes a succession of poor and unjustified points, badly expressed and spelt. What does 'his need but remorse to change' mean? How does the 'alliteration on big boy' emphasise 'how time has left him'? There is nothing for an examiner to reward in a paragraph like this and, in fact, little to reward in the answer as a whole.

'The Oven Bird' is a form a sonnet starting mono selabically it changes from iambic pentametre and back this emphaises on how Frost writes about change and timing.

e The candidate correctly identifies 'The Oven Bird' as a sonnet but does not move beyond this identification. No evidence is offered to support the dubious points about the change in metre and the candidate's experiments with English spelling continue ('mono selabically' for 'monosyllabically', 'pentametre' for 'pentameter' and 'emphaises' for 'emphasises').

Frost metaphoric meaning help us more to distinguish his ideas on time and change. 'Oven Bird' concentrates on his time to diminish whereas 'Out, Out —' concentrates on his wanting not to have to change and grow up.

e **Overall, this is a misguided and muddled attempt at answering the question. There is only the occasional point of understanding that an examiner can credit. The majority of the answer is poor, though there is an occasional focus on the question. It would be awarded 6 marks, a U grade, and has been included in this guide as an example of *what not to do*.**